The Way Things Were

The Way Things Were

Days of My Life

Emma Garrett Williams

FROM 1918 TO THE PRESENT

authorHOUSE®

AuthorHouse™
1663 Liberty Drive
Bloomington, IN 47403
www.authorhouse.com
Phone: 1-800-839-8640

Published by AuthorHouse   10/03/2012

ISBN: 978-1-4685-8509-4 (sc)
ISBN: 978-1-4685-8508-7 (e)

Library of Congress Control Number: 2012907215

Any people depicted in stock imagery provided by Thinkstock are models, and such images are being used for illustrative purposes only.
Certain stock imagery © Thinkstock.

This book is printed on acid-free paper.

Because of the dynamic nature of the Internet, any web addresses or links contained in this book may have changed since publication and may no longer be valid. The views expressed in this work are solely those of the author and do not necessarily reflect the views of the publisher, and the publisher hereby disclaims any responsibility for them.

CONTENTS

DAVE T. GARRETT

It all begins with the history of my Grandfather and Grandmother Dave Thomas Garrett's and Sarah Davis Garrett.

Tom Garrett married Sarah Davis Garrett and lived in Alabama. Betty Wilberly, Tom Garrett' grandmother lived to be 102 years old. She had several children; Robert, Lillie Bell, Estell, and Mamie.

Tom Garrett and Sarah Davis Garrett were the parents of two children Lillie Bell and Dave Samuel Garrett.

Lillie Bell had two boys, Sylvester Simmons of New Orleans and Dave Simmons of Los Angeles, California. Sylvester had 5 children, Dave had 2 children.

Dave Samuel Garrett became a minister and married Josephine Robinson Garrett. They met and lived in Waveland, Mississippi. Dave and Josephine had 14 children. Their children are Rudolph, Bessie, Comeail, Emma Lee, Mary, Samuel, Josephine Lucille, Andrew, Celestine, Thomas, Nathaniel and Ella Mae and two other children (Twins) that died at birth.

Rudolph (January 3, 1913-December 3, 1981) married Rosa Lee Lewis of New Orleans, Louisiana and had four children, Barbara, Rudolph Jr., Clifton and Edward. Rudolph M. Garrett worked as an engineer for Southern Pacific Railroad and lived in San Francisco, California.

Bessie (1912-1928) died at the young age of 18.

Comeail (May 10, 1916-October 30, 1958) married Rev. Manson Peters of Hub, Mississippi; they had three children, Gladys Peters Mango, Manson Peters Jr. and Rev. Donald Peters.

Emma Lee (February 17, 1918-Present) married Rev. James Wilson of Shreveport, Louisiana and Julius Williams of Jackson, Mississippi; they had nine children, Mary Elizabeth, Florence, Talibah (Naomi), James, Doris, Sharron, Deborah, Ezra Addon and Leon (Speedy).

Mary (March 4, 1920-July 21, 1997) married Amos Failey of Wiggins, Mississippi; they had one daughter Marva. Mary E. Garrett Fairley a graduate of Valena C. Jones High School of Bay St. Louis Mississippi, and a graduate of Coinson School of Nursing Booker T. Washington in New Orleans Louisiana. She was a LPN and served as State President of Louisiana Nurses Association and was on the Board of the National Association of Nurses. She was an active and devoted member of Peck Methodist Church, Chairman of the Pastor Parish Relations Nominating Committee, Delegate to the Annual Conference, and a member of the Commission of Education.

Samuel (June 17, 1921-December 21, 1993) married Doris Baker of Pass Christian, Mississippi; they had two sons, Orlando and Samuel Jr. Samuel Dave Garrett served several years in the United State Army. Samuel's two sons: Orlando and Samuel D. Garrett Jr. also served in the Military.

Josephine Lucille (February 6, 1923-Deceased 2004) married Rev. John W. Bryant of New Orleans, Louisiana; they had eight children, Consuella "Connie", Katherine, Juanita, Joanne, Antoinette, John Jr., Keith and Dave. She was an active member in the Communion Stewards of the United Methodist Church. Josephine Lucille Garrett Bryant worked at DePaul Hospital for many years as a Social Worker, and also at the Rainbow Brite Learning Center. She loved her family and friends but most of all she loved God.

Andrew never married and had no children. Andrew B. Garrett (Deceased, 1997). Andrew was a very loving and caring individual with lots of love to give his family and friends. Painting and mechanic were two of Andrew's many skills. "We will miss his jokes and laughter."

Celestine (March 6, 1924-Present) married John W. Matthew of Van Cleave, Mississippi; they had seven children, John Jr., Charles, Michael, Lisa, Byron, Eric and Mark.

Thomas (July 28, 1928-December 6, 2006) married Minnie of Arkansas and Irene of California; they had eleven children, Johnnie, Louise, Evelyn, Levi, Gregory, Thomas Jr., Lawrence, Zetta, Zee, Humphrey and Jennie.

Nathaniel (July 1, 1930-Present) married Ora Lee Willingham of Waveland, Mississippi; they had six children, Jacqueline, Nathaniel Jr., Anthony, Denise, Natalie and Timothy.

Ella Mae (April 2, 1935-Present) married Homer Gregory of California and Willie Hankton of California; they had eleven children; Diane, Mark, Angie, Wendell, Diane, Anthony, Nathan, Nathaniel, Lawrence and Alexander and one other girl.

JOHNSON FAMILY
(DECEDENTS OF
SARA DAVIS GARRETT)

Mamie Wilberly married Miles Johnson of Waveland, Mississippi: they had four children, Thomas, Vivian, Sam and Calvin.

Thomas Johnson married Ada of New Orleans Louisiana and they had one son; Thomas Jr.

Vivian Johnson married James McKimley of New Orleans, Louisiana and they had eight children; James, John, Ester Mae, Alexander, Roosevelt, Vivian (name after her Mother), Edward and Roy Lee.

Calvin Johnson did not have any children.

Sam Johnson married Lillian of New Orleans, Louisiana and they had six children; Estell, Ruth Mae, Dorothy Lee, Lillian, Helen, Emanuel and Samuel.

Estell did not have any children.

Ruth Mae married Andrew Lee Collins of Waveland Mississippi and they had one daughter, Shirley Collins.

Dorothy Lee married Mr. George they had one son. Dorothy Johnson-George was born in Biloxi, Mississippi to the late Sam and Lillian Johnson on September 25, 1933. Dorothy leaves to cherish her memory her son George Lee Slack Jr., four sisters, Ruth Mae Johnson Collins, Helen Johnson Antoine, and Lillian Johnson of Louisiana, also two brothers, Samuel Johnson and Emanuel Johnson, a host of nieces and nephews and other loving relatives and friends.

Lillian married Mr. Mallary of New Orleans, Louisiana and they had five children.

Helen married Sylvester Antoine and had ten children. (Children's names were unknown).

Emanuel married (Wife name unknown) and had seven children. (Children's names are unknown)

Samuel (wife and number of children are unknown)

Dave T. Garret's other relatives; the Macemore's and Wilberly's reside in Gulfport Mississippi.

JOSEPHINE ROBINSON GARRETT DECEDENTS (DAVE S. GARRETT'S WIFE)

Caroline Martin had four girls and one boy; Anna Martin Stull, Lizzie Martin Robinson, Mary Martin Jones, Callie Martin Banks and son James (Jim).

Lizzie Martin Robinson the daughter of Caroline Martin lived in a little town north of Jackson, Louisiana called Vidalia.

The family lived on a plantation until Anna Martin married John Stull, one of the plantation owner's sons.

Anna and John moved to New Orleans, Louisiana and they had one daughter Lillian.

Lillian married Adam Harris Sr. and the couple had eight children; Lillian her oldest and namesake, Adam Jr., Odeal, Sedona, Minnie, Anna Rose, Joyce and John. Lillian S. Harris daughter of the late John and Anna Stull of New Orleans and sister of Lizzie Robinson leaves to cherish her memory her children, a host of grandchildren and one cousin.

Lillian's first born Lillian (name after her mother) married Dave Anderson, they had no children.

Adam Jr. married Vivian of New Orleans and had five children.

Minnie married Samuel Johnson and they also had no children.

Odeal married Rev. Lee Morris of Waveland, Mississippi and they had nine children. Odeal was born in New Orleans, Louisiana. Odeal loved the Lord was an active member of her church.

Sedona Married John Lemay and they had seven children.

Joyce married Mr. Leroy Nelson and to that union had one daughter. Joyce E. was born on April 9, 1937 in Waveland, Mississippi. She later married Hilliard Mercer, who preceded her in death. And they had eight children. She leaves to cherish her memory two brothers Adam Harris Jr. and John Harris and one daughter Lisa Mercer. Over her life, she served faithfully at St Rock United Methodist Church in Waveland, Mississippi and served on the Food and Nutrition Committee.

John married Clement Goldsmith and had one child. John Harris was born in New Orleans, Louisiana to the late Adam and Lillian Harris. He leaves to cherish his memory on daughter, sisters and a host of nieces, nephews, cousins and friends.

After moving to New Orleans, Anna help Mary and her husband Jo Jones leave the plantation.

Mary then sent for Lizzie and her husband Andrew Robinson; Jim and Callie soon followed. Callie married Mr. Banks of New Orleans; Jim married Mord also of New Orleans. After several years the family relocated to Waveland, Mississippi on the Gulf Coast, southeast of New Orleans.

James (Jim) Morton had two sons; James Jr. and Edgar. The son's never married.

Lizzie Morton Robinson married Andrew Robinson and had only one child, Josephine Robinson who married Dave T. Garrett of Alabama.

REV. AND MRS. DAVE S. GARRETT

Rev. Dave S. Garrett a native of Montgomery, Alabama was married to Josephine Robinson of Jackson, Louisiana. The union was blessed with fourteen children. The Family lived for years in Hancock County. In 1914, Dave became the first African American mailman. Dave's career spanned a range of opportunities including county government advisor, youth counselor, ice delivery man and garbage collector. He was a member of Little Zion Baptist Church where he was ordained a minister. He then served as Pastor of Mount Chapel Baptist Church. Rev. Garrett returned with his wife to Little Zion Baptist Church as the Pastor until their death in October of 1958.

A TRAGIC DAY
WAVELAND MAN EIGHTH VICTIM OF AUTO CRASH

The death of Anthony Bridges, 30 year old Waveland Negro, at about 3:30 p.m. October 30, 1958 brought to a total of eight killed as a result of injuries suffered in a two car collision October 26 on old US-90 at Nicholson Avenue intersection. Bridges was the driver of the car which struck broadside an auto carrying seven Negroes, all of whom were killed instantly. Bridges was taken to Hancock County Hospital and transferred to Memorial Hospital at Gulfport for treatment of two broken legs, a broken back and neck injuries. His condition was listed as poor until his death. The other dead were: The Rev. Dave Garrett 69, of Waveland and Pastor of the Little Zion Baptist Church, Mrs. Josephine Garrett 68, his wife, Benjamin Walker 62, Rev. Garrett's brother-in-law, Mrs. Little Belle Walker 61 his wife and sister of Rev. Garrett, Rev. Manson Peters 45, the Pastor of St. Rock Methodist Church in Middletown Community and a son-in-law of Rev. Garrett; Mrs. Comeail Garrett Peters, his wife and a daughter of Rev. Garrett; Rev. Howard L. King 45, an alternate Pastor of the Little Zion Baptist Church. Rev. King was the driver of the other car, and his six passengers apparently were traveling east on US 90.

LILLIE BELL WALKER GARRETT

Lillie Bell Walker Garrett, the sister of Rev. Dave Garrett born in Montgomery Alabama to Tommy and Mary Davis Garrett had one daughter and two sons.

left to right:

Nathaniel Garrett, Josephine Garrett, Mary Garrett

left to right: Minnie Garrett, child-unknown,
Mary Jones, Lizzie Robinson

left to right: John Matthews, Samuel Garrett,
Lucille Garrett, Andrew Garrett

left to right: child unknown, Celestine Garrett, Minnie Garrett,
Emma Garrett, Andrew Garrett, Ora Lee Garrett, Nathaniel
Garrett, Samuel Garrett, Josephine Garrett, Lucille Garrett, Dave
Garrett, child unknown.

DAYS OF MY LIFE

In the year of 1918 on February 17 Emma L Garrett was born to the late Reverend Dave S. Garrett and the late Josephine Robinson Garrett in a little town called Waveland Mississippi, southeast of Louisiana. I'm the fourth (4) of Fourteen (14) children.

At a young age I went to live with my grandmother Lizzie Robinson until I was about (10) years old. My grandmother and I had lots of fun doing things together, like the walks we took and the stories she told me about her life and growing up in Louisiana, a little place called Byseria south of Jackson Louisiana were she lived and work on a plantation.

We attended Church and Sunday school every Sunday. Saturday nights were reserved for church programs. During the week we work most of the time. We traveled by my grandfather's horses and buggy.

YOUTH IN WAVELAND

My grandparents and I live on St Joseph Street in Waveland Mississippi in a three (3) bed room home and as of July 1999 the home was still there. It's about two-hundred (200) years old.

Here are some memorable times spent with my grandmother; we picked berries, ground coffee, baked pies, took long walks through the woods, talk and look at all the different birds. It was a good life. The type of work we did was cooking and making beds for other people.

In 1926 my grandfather passed away, one year later my grandmother and I went to live with my parents and all my siblings at 212 Broad Street in Waveland. At that time I was in high school, my teacher was Ms Ester Breaux and I received my first certification to go to college but I was not able to go because there were so many of my siblings to take care of. So I had to stay and help my mother do domestic work to take care of all of us.

RESPONSIBILITIES

My dream to go to college and become a school teacher was all over so I thought. I cried every morning because my dream of going to college did not seem possible. Grandmother Lizzie would say Emma one day you will be able to go, just hold on to your dream and keep it close to your heart. Now "Le" be a good girl and help your mother because she works so hard to keep you all together. My mother worked hard supporting the family because to my father was ill most of the time. My mother and I worked together until I was 18. One day mother said to me, you know the family next door needs someone to help out. So I ask please may I go and see if she would let me help and mother said yes and make sure you thank her. I said yes ma'am, I know what to do because you taught me all the things I need to know like cooking and cleaning. I got the job, she paid me six (6) dollars a week in the summer but when her sister and family came over she gave me one (1) dollars more. I worked there for Five (5) years. Doing that time I was able to buy three (3) lots of land from McDonald for $75.00 a lot a total of $275.00 for all three lots. I paid $3.00 a week until it was paid off. I soon had a little house built next door to my mother's home; it had three (3) bed rooms, kitchen, bath and living room, my first home.

MARRIAGES

In 1937 I married the late James L. Collins, from this married we had two (2) children. We divorces two years later and I move to Montgomery Alabama where I work for one year then move to New Orleans, Louisiana. I was employed as a cook for Charity Hospital in New Orleans where my dream was about to come to life. First I met and married the late Rev James W Wilson, from this marriage there were six (6) children. He was a United Methodist Minister.

REV. DR. JAMES WILLIAM WILSON SR.

Rev. Dr. James William Wilson Sr. LL.B., DD of Shreveport, Louisiana received his BA from Rust College in Holly Springs, Mississippi and his Doctor of Divinity from Gammon Theological Seminary, Atlanta, Georgia in 1952, his Bachelor of Law from Blackstone School of Law (Chicago, IL) in 1958. Rev Wilson was ordained in 1955 to the United Methodist Church. His first ministry assignment was in Slidell, Louisiana. Later in his service to God he became District Superintendent and then Treasurer of the Louisiana United Methodist Church Conference. He was a member of 128 FFAM where he served as Post Master.

DREAMS ON ITS WAY

My dream was on its way when we relocated to Holly Springs Mississippi, where we both were able to attend Rust College. I became the queen of Rust my junior year and started my student teaching where I worked for the government teaching G.I.'s While at Rust College I was able to travel all around the Mississippi Delta where I observed and learned so much about how other people lived in those days. Some homes had no windows or doors, cotton for miles, a store every now and then, no schools and a few churches. There were no cars only wagons, cows, horses and other farm animals. Lots of fresh food and dirt streets.

The little towns were very quiet. The people were very religious and happy. I fell in love with them and they treated me as one of their own. The people always talked about God in their lives. I travel by bus and train across the country. It was very hard to travel in those days. It was a wonderful experience to travel and talk with the people, most

of all the children. My dream then began to come alive. There was so much I wanted to do. I was able to touch so many young people lives.

I wrote my thesis on rural education. James and I both received our Bachelor of Science from Rust College.

In 1949 I received my second degree in General Education. I attended North Western University in Natchitoches, Louisiana where I received my BA in Fine Art and Children Literature. In 1954 I received a Master's Degree in Physical Education and Child Psychology from Xavier University of New Orleans, Louisiana. Rev. James W. Wilson received his Doctor of Divinity from Gammon Theological Seminary in Atlanta, GA. Rev. Wilson's first ministry assignment was in Slidell, LA, where we lived for five years, then to Algiers, LA off to Mansfield for one year, off too Natchitoches, LA for 2 years, then Shreveport, LA, and then to New Orleans. He became the United Methodist District Superintendent for Baton Rouge District. I became the first Lady of the Baton Rouge District and we travel every weekend too his churches. The children and I traveled all over Louisiana, hundreds of miles, returning home to Waveland MS by Sunday night and preparing for work and school the next day.

That tragic day in October 1958, my father, mother, sister, brother in law, uncle and aunt were killed in a car accident. It was so divesting that I stop working for two weeks. During that summer Bishop R.N Brooks sent me to Gulfside Assembly in Waveland, MS to work with his wife to open up the new hotel Brook End which is now call the End. In August of that year I was hired at Valena C. Jones in Bay St Louis MS as a fourth grade teacher. Tyrone Sexton was the principles at that time. What a year I had, my dream came alive, I owe it all to GOD and my grandmother Lizzie for the trust she had in me. It was the happiest time of my life. We continue to live in Waveland, where the children enjoyed living in a rural community. I was ready to build a larger home for my family right across the street from the first home and my mother's home. It had 4 bedrooms, 2 baths, separate living & family room and a formal dining room large enough to house two dining tables.

When Rev. Wilson wanted a divorce I granted it. It took a lot out of me to do this, but I remembered what my mother and grandmother taught me, to be strong and stay with the lord. The next year I went to work in Marion County were I fell very ill at the state meeting, in Jackson, MS. I was taken to the Baptist Hospital in Jackson and Rev. Wilson was called. He brought me to Slidell where he was staying and I could not work for one year. My sister Mary E Garrett Fairley took care of me. When I recovered I went back to work. While attending a church affair, I met Mr. J.P. Johnson as we talked he said, "I remember you from my days at Rust College, you were our queen", I said yes I was, your name is Mrs. Wilson you are JW's wife. Reverend Wilson was sometimes called JW. I gave him a smile and said yes. Mr. Johnson was principle of George W. Carver High & Elementary School in Picayune, MS. He said to me, "I need a third grade teacher and he hired me. I worked there for twenty five (25) years. The Lord blessed me to raise all my children and send them to high school and on to college. My dreams were fulfilled, the prayer I prayed to God every day was answered.

One week I was driving with my son-in-law Louis Washington on the Gulf Coast, showing him the beauty of the coast as he had never seen before. That's were I meet the late Rev Julius Williams of Jackson, MS. I ask myself why this had to happen, he was divorce, a very nice man, we had a lot in common and as we talked about our pass and things we would like to do in life, three (3) month later we were married in Jackson, MS at his home church by Rev Matthews his pastor.

This was a happy time in my life because I know that God had brought us together. I was over flowing with all my dreams, no matter what happen in my life I know I was bless. Rev Williams went back to school at Thelma University in Atlanta, GA where he received his minister degree. He was a minister in the Gulfside United Methodist Church District.

Rev Williams served in the US Navy as Steward Mate First Class on the USS Saratoga. We attended several ship reunions where we enjoyed visiting friends and shipmates. I continued to live in Waveland, a thirty five (35) miles commute one way to Picayune on a two lane road with farm animals crossing at any moment.

REV. JULIUS WILLIAMS SR.

Rev. Julius Williams Sr. a graduate of Candler School of Theology, Emory University, Atlanta, Georgia. Julius was ordained a minister by The United Methodist Church in 1974 (The Mississippi Conference). He pastored seven churches. He was the father of four children and stepfather of seven.

George W. Carver Elementary, Picayune, MS

SCHOOL EVENTS

While at Carver I organized several plays and operetta's the last one was "Season of Happiness"

Sharron my 6th child played the part of Molly with Mrs. Gulf on the piano, I directed the play. With my Art background, I designed all the school Floats, took first place with my creativity for "Old Lady in a Shoe" and honorable mention for "Black Beauty". My class was voted the top class in the school and we had so much fun creating things.

The children love me; some still write and call me as of today. The school is now a museum. In the museum there is a picture of me and my third grade class.

I was never late for school, we only had one car so I dropped Julius off for work, and continue on to school, I had to attend after school programs with the older children, pick up Julius, drive thirty five (35) miles back home. After a hard long day I still had to cook, wash, help the children with their home work, study, make a lesson plan for the next day, grade papers and off to bed around 10:00pm most night. Get back up and ready to go about 6:00am to start the next day. After five (5) years the three youngest children were old enough to be enrolled in a private school in Waveland. They were picked up each morning by taxi. A private sitter took care of them until we returned in the evening. We had many long days and spent a lot of time together. It was enjoyable most days having the family together and helping each other.

Time passed quickly, the older children begin their own lives, Florence move to California and a few years later Elizabeth moved there also. Talibah (Naomi) and James were in college, leaving the five (5) youngest children home with me. That was Doris, Sharron, Deborah, Ezra (Addon) and Leon (Speedy).

MOVED TO CALIFORNIA

In 1975 Julius and I moved to California and lived with Elizabeth a while. Then we rented a place of our own. As I waited for Sacramento to send my certification papers to teach in California, I got a job with San Francisco General Hospital. I worked for the state of California teaching fifth and six grades for ten years and retired at the age of 77. I was so busy in California, When I retired from teaching school and moved from San Francisco to Oakland, bought a home at 2424 106th Ave Oakland, CA.

Then I open a pre-school called Radian Day Care & Pre-School with forty Children from ages 0-6 years old. My girls work with me and soon we opened Lee's Creole Cuisine, this was Leon joy. I was very active in Grace United Methodist Church, Rev John Benison pastor. At Grace United I spear-headed the California National Pre-Teen in May 1989 and also the Calendar of Tea. We relocated to Brooke Methodist Episcopal Church where I was appointed office of the Steward Board, President Vacation Bible School where I received certificates and awards from the pastor Rev Allen L Williams. On my seventh fifth

(75) birthday my children's gave me a surprise birthday party at the Holiday Inn in Oakland which I really did enjoy. It was one of the best parties I ever had, "what a time we had". In 1990 I close Radian Day Care and Lee's Creole Cuisine and relocated to Peoria AZ were Julius and I join United with Christ Our Redeemer Methodist Church under Pastor Paulette D. Paytee, the church is now call My Father House Christians Church. I am one of the church board members and president of the Women Ministry.

FAMILY REUNION

In 1998 I organized our second Garrett Family Reunion which was held at Gulf side in Waveland. The theme was (For God so loved the world that He gave His only begotten Son, that whosoever believeth in Him should not perish, but have eternal life.) John 3:16. The T-shirts were gray with the Bible on front in honor of my father.

We also had a book made of the Garrett Family Generations. What a turn out it was, over one hundred family members were there.

God blessed me again in July 2000 to be able to organize another Family Reunion, this time it was with the Garrett and Johnson Family. This reunion was held at the Holiday Inn in Waveland and its theme was (Giving God to Glory). The T-shirt were white again we use the bible in honor of our father because he was a Minister. We had a great time. Again in 2004 God blessed me to be able to do one more reunion. This time it was a larger reunion with the Garrett, Johnson and Harris Family which was held at the Coastal Inn, the theme was (Walking with God). A book was designed to honor all the deceased family members. Now it was time for the young members of the family to take over and organize the family reunion.

Julius passed in 1999 and Leon and I decided to down side our home because it was just the two of us. I got busy and found a smaller home for us. I purchased the home I live in today, located at 10211 78th Lane Peoria AZ.

Leon passed in 2003. That was very hard for me first Julius then Leon but God saw me through it all. Within six months of Leon passing I moved to Vista Del Rio at 94 Drive Peoria AZ a senior living facility, this is what Leon wanted me to do. I spent all my time traveling, reading, writing, arts and craft and looking after my friends, Mildred and Lonnie.

We had fun doing things together and going to church when I could get a ride. Radian would pick me up for church or I stayed with Deborah on Saturday night and went with her and her family. This was the only time I wished I had a car because it was so hard for me to get around.

Vista Del Rio was nice, lots of actives to do, but I missed the children, grandchildren and great grandchildren. As a mother of nine (9) with twenty-one (21) grand children thirty (30) great grand children and three (3) great great-grandchildren how could I not miss all of that. God has giving me a wonderful life to be able to see and enjoy all of them.

My best friends: Mary Benton, Mary Lu Hamilton and Mable Brown all of California, we called each other every weekend. The only close friend I had in Waveland was Helen Hargett and she passed some years ago.

HURRICANE

In August 2005 there was a Harris Family Reunion which I did attended and I was able to meet lots of cousins that I had not seen in a long, long time and some new ones. Elizabeth and her children had moved back to Bay St. Louis, Mississippi, so I had the opportunity to stay with them. While I was in Waveland and Bay St. Louis we got news that Hurricane Katrina would hit on Monday. We got busy trying to prepare for it and there were so many things to do. During this time many people lives were disturbed, children crying, and things were just a mess. Elizabeth decided to stay home, her children left and went to Montgomery Alabama. My nephew Manson Peterson said I need to leave also, so he took his wife and me to Brookhaven MS. The next day we went back to Waveland/ Bay St. Louis to see about Elizabeth and Manson's home that we left behind. When we arrived we found all the homes, stores, churches and trees destroyed. The area looked like a battle zone. I began to live hurricane Camille all over again in my mind. I thought about how my home was destroyed, trees down, the Borax family of five (5) killed, how other people and children all died, it was a terrifying feeling. But Katrina was the worse hurricane I have ever seen in my life and I've been through several hurricanes but none like this.

Shortly after Katrina pass people everywhere were crying for help—HELP, someone please HELP us, this day I will never forget babies crying and there was nowhere to go for help. I walked the streets of Waveland trying to get help for people but I just could not do it. So I prayed and prayed, walk and walk until someone came, as I began to wear down a car drove up. I asked the man in the car where he was going. He said Jackson; I ask if I could get a ride with him, off to Jackson we went. Julius family lived in Jackson. The Lord was with me every day, all I could see was devastation from the storm and people now homeless, I prayed and prayed. I hoped that my family in New Orleans got out and were alive. Thanks to God they all did and were safe. By October I was able to go home, back to Peoria, AZ and what a happy day that was for me and my children. After all that, I see how bless I am with my children looking after me all the time.

ALL MY CHILDREN

Radian my granddaughter (Doris older daughter) was my driver and she took me all around Arizona. She was so good to me. Now she is married and lives in North Carolina, Tailbah makes sure I have all my medication. Sharron keeps me flying from city to city (smile). James calls to see if I'm ok and have money and/or food. Debbie calls every day to keep me up on the family news (smile) and we go to church together on Sunday. She is married to Leonard, Johnson who helps me however he can.

Ezra is my quiet child who does his own thing, what every that may be, he helps me as much as he can. Elizabeth and I talk every Sunday night for hours, she is working to rebuild St Rock United Methodist Church. St. Rock was the church of my grandmother Lizzie and her sister; it was built in the nineteen hundreds. Elizabeth is doing a wonderful job with that project. Doris my phone girl, oh how we could talk, she really made me laugh about the children, her son La Jewell (my best friend, always phoned with a story to tell). I finally move back to my home at 10211 78th Lane from Vista Del Ri0, the senior living facility. I'm 94 years old now and I feel very good, no real health problems at this time (just old) smile. The children pay to have my house cleaned every two week. I'm so thankful for that because I am not able to do some of the things that need to be done around the house. I thank God for all my blessing and my children. My children, grandchildren, great grand children and great great grand children are my life. Oh how I love them all in their own unique ways.

My grandsons De'Andre, De'Allo and Ja'man are on the wrong road of life. But God will take care of them and change their lives. I pray every day and asked God to keep watch over them. We all fall down in life but we can get back up again. I write to them every day or so I ask God to let me see them again before my days are over.

MY DAILY EVENTS

I have my church, I'm still doing ministry, taking care of the Laments for Communion each first Sunday. My day starts off with a prayer, reading my bible, my favorite chapter is Psalm 86, then I take a walk around the park, about two (2) miles, feed the birds, walk down the street to the mail box, back in the house for breakfast, by this time it's 9:00am, now it's time for Debbie to start calling. If I have a doctor's appointment, I take the Peoria Transit and off I go. Back home more call from Debbie and more call from Debbie (smile) in between all Debbie calls I get, Doris, Sharron, James, Taliba and sometime Addon, then all the grand children, its dinner time, watch some TV and at 9:00pm off to bed.

Some days are very blue for me, I start to think about the lost of my children Florence first, then on Oct 28 Speedy passed, Oh how I miss him, on 16th February 2009 Doris was kill in a car accidence on her way home from my birthday party the children gave me for my 92nd birthday, we had so much fun. Doris would call me every day and I miss her calls. That same year in July we had another family reunion, this one at the home of Lisa Moore in New Orleans, LA, it was very good, most of the families were represented and over a hundred people were there. 2009 was a busy year for me, I took my first cruise on the Carnival Cruise Line, had dinner with the captain of the ship, what a time we had. We also stopped in Jacksonville, FL that was fun to.

In September 2009 my great niece Gina Batiste (grand daughter of my brother Nathaniel Garrett) got married in New Orleans and I stayed with my great nephew Bernard Hays for a week, we had a glories time.

GOD'S GOODNESS

"GOD IS GOOD". Give thanks to the Lord, for he is good, for his mercy endures forever. I called on the Lord in my distress, the Lord answered me and set me in a broad place; the Lord is on my side, I will not fear. What can man do to me? The Lord is there for me among those who help me. Therefore I shall see my desire on those who hate me. It is better to trust in the Lord then to put confidence in man. You pushed me violently that I might fall but the Lord helped me. The Lord is my strength and song. He has become my salvation. The right hand of the Lord does valiantly. I shall not die, but live and declare the works of the Lord. The Lord has chastened me severely but he has not given me over to death. Open the gate of righteousness I will go through them, and I will praise the Lord and enter through the gates of righteousness. I pray O Lord I pray send more prosperity, you are my God and I will praise you. Oh give thanks to the Lord for he is good for His mercy endures forever.

My Love

From top left to right: Florence, Sharron, Ezra (Addon), James Jr.,
Leon Speedy, Talibah (Naomi), bottom left Deborah, Elizabeth and Doris

Now let me give you some history of my children as you know I'm the
mother of nine (9), they are the joy of my life in their own individual
way, In their unique way they can keep a smile on my face ever day.

Mary Elizabeth (Washington) Roberts

Elizabeth was born the 14th day of August in New Orleans LA; she attended Book T Washington High School in New Orleans. She graduated college from Grambling University. Elizabeth is the mother of five (5) Louis Jr., Carol, William, Gina and Elisha, also a grandmother of nine (9). Elizabeth was a school teacher, Librarian and interior designer with many other talents. She loved traveling to Switzerland, France, Austria and Germany. A few of her hobbies is are sewing building, panting and gardening.

Elizabeth now lives in Bay St. Louis with her children and grand children.

Florence Rosa Lee Davidson

Florence was born in New Orleans, LA the 28th day of December. She attended St. Rose delima High School in Bay St. Louis, MS. She received her business degree at Straight Business College in New Orleans. She worked in nursing for several years, open a foster care home for young children in Napa, CA where she lived. Florence is the mother of four (4) children; Charlotte, Zina, Elmira and De'Allo, grandmother of seven (7). Florence loved children and people, she also had a love for dogs and cats. Until she pass in 1992, Florence and I would laugh and talk every night at 10:00 pm, my love for her goes on, but God loved her more.

Talibah (Naomi) Wilson Al-Rafiq

Talibah is my third child, she was born on February 11th in Atlanta, GA. She graduated from George W. Carver High in Picayune MS. Talibah received her BA degree from Dillard University in New Orleans in Psychology and Education, Master in Business Management, and her Doctorate Degree in Psychology. Talibah has traveled the world, places like Austria, Germany, Fiji, Japan, China, France, Russia, Switzerland and more. She is married to Ajamu Al-Rafiq, they have no children. Talibah and Ajamu own California Cashmere. The company was founded in 1990, located in the Sierra Foothills of Calaveras County, some 600 meters above sea level, 256 kilometers north-east of San Francisco, in the heart of California's 1849 "Gold Rush" region. California Cashmere Company does business internationally. The company offers cashmere yarn knitwear, classes, farm tours and livestock. California Cashmere Company is only commercial custom cashmere dehairer in the United States. In 1996 they imported the technology from China for this process. Talibah has many talents; she knits, sews, gardens, creates all their marketing materials and serves on numerous non-profit boards in her community. I visit the 240 acre farm often. It is rewarding to feed the animals and help in the processing mill. At day's end we sit around the kitchen table and enjoy one of her farm fresh country dinners. Can't wait for my next trip.

James William Wilson Jr.

James is my first son and fourth child, born in New Orleans, LA on March 20th. He also graduated from George W. Carver High in Picayune, MS; in high school he played the trumpet in the marching band. He received his BS degree in Marketing from Southern University in Baton Rouge, LA. James is a Procurement Specialist for a Medical Device Company. He is single, lives in Sunnyvale, CA and doesn't have any children. James still plays the trumpet and is always on the go. His career has taken him to Spain, Costa Rico, Scotland, Whales, London, Amsterdam and many states in the U.S. and more. James loves his family.

Doris Marie Wilson

My sweet Doris was born August 3rd in New Orleans, LA a graduated of Picayune Memorial High School in Picayune MS. Doris also is a graduated of Merritt College in Oakland CA; she holds two business degrees, Business Administration from Southwest Business College in Hayward CA, the other in Accounting from Heald Business College in San Francisco CA. Doris hobbies were serving, panting and reading. She is the mother of four (4) La'Jewell, Radian, De'Andre and Anchilitia (Oh! how she loved her children), the grandmother of ten (10). Doris passed in February 2009, she love life, her family and people.

Sharron A. Wilson Brown

This is my unique child; she was born on the 8th day of February in Slidell LA. She attended Our Lady of Academy in Waveland, MS and graduated from Abraham Lincoln High School in San Francisco CA. She attended Merritt College in Oakland, CA and received a degree in Biology and Art. Sharron attended Oakland College of Dental-Nurse; she worked as a nurse for 25 years, Emergency Medical Technician for 3 years. Sharron is very active in her church, she serves on the Usher Board, teaches a Youth Mission Class and Ministry Leader for the Health & Wellness Team. Sharron loves traveling the world; Fiji, Japan, China, Hawaii, Canada and Philippine. There are so many that I can't keep up. Her hobbies included horse back riding, flower arrangement, sign language, community service, traveling and science. She is the mother of three (3) Alexeev Sr., Robert III and Kadena. She is the grandmother of four (4). Sharron would like to own and operate a Funeral Home business in the near future (remember I said my unique child) you see why.

Deborah Wilson Johnson

Deborah was born in Gulfport MS on April 27th; she too graduated from Abraham Lincoln High School in San Francisco CA. She attended Grambling University where she received her degree in Business. Deborah is also very active in the church, she sings in the Choir, serves on the Usher Board and President of the Praised Dance Ministry. She enjoys basketball, football and her family. Deborah favorite third grade saying was; 'hit the road jack'. Deborah is married to Rev Leonard Johnson, she is the mother of three (3) Najla, Ja'Mon and A'jona and a resident of Peoria AZ

Ezra Addon Wilson

On January 4th Ezra was born in New Orleans, LA. He graduated Castlemount High School in Oakland CA. He attended Grambling University where he studied Education and Woodshop. In high school and college, Ezra was outstanding in Track, Football and the Boxing Teams. As of today he still loves the sports. Ezra lives in Sacramento, CA, married and the father of two (2) Emily and Ezekiel and the grandfather of one (1).

Leon (Le'Jon) Williams

Leon (Speedy) my baby, he was born in Picayune Mississippi on January 24, 1966 at Crosby Hospital. He graduated from Rockbridge High School in Oakland, CA. He attended Firm College of Art's and Designs in San Francisco, CA. Leon open up LeJon Tailoring Shop in downtown Oakland were he made men and woman clothing. I must say he was good at it; he made dresses for his sisters and me. He always tried to keep the family together with Sunday meals. Leon loved his family, he directed the choir at Grace United Methodist Church in Oakland CA. When we move to Peoria, AZ, Leon worked for the Men Warehouse as a wardrobe consultant for five (5) years. He was awarded Executive Commute, Wardrobe Consultant of The Year, he was recognized for his work with the Josephine Baker Doty

Fashion Show and was awarded seven models to model his clothing designs. He received all type of certificates and awards from Men Warehouse. Leon become ill and passed on October 24 2003, every one who knew him as Speedy love him. Speedy was his nickname and he was a devoted and loving person. Sharron had her own name for him, which was Bud (Oh how she loved him!!). Leon (Speedy) loved his church and his pastor, but God loved him BEST.

MY WORK DAY'S PICTURES

Here are some of my works day's pictures

School Day

Radian Day Care and Pre School

San Francisco Department
of Public Health

TRADEGY

On February 16, 2009, Doris went home to be with the Lord, on July 27, 2010 her son LeJewell also went home to be with the Lord; this was a hard time for me. The pressure of all of this and being 93 years young was extreme. I suffered a light heart attack on September 23, 2010 and was hospitalize for five (5) days. Oh how my God took good care of me with the help of my children, I made it through it. I'm here today and I can truly say I could not have made it without Him or them. Each of my children stayed with me for a week at a time. I had five weeks of my children being with me and that was a pleasure. I loved every moment of it. I did not feel sick, not one time with all the love from the children, nieces, nephew, my pastor and church family being there for me at any time. God laid down his life for us so we can have life, we can help give life back to the ones we love. As mothers we raise our children to give back love to each other. I will soon be 95 years old on February 17, 2013 as I stand here today with the power of God, I stand strong as I fight a good fight of faith.

Remember if you get knock down don't stay down get back up, learn to do as David, encourage yourself in the Lord. God has destined you to live a life of victory, but you must do your part, in all of this. Make a firm decision that no matter what come your way or against you in life, keep standing on the side of the Lord. Be happy with who you are and what God made of you.

This book was is a synopsis of the life and works of Emma Lee Garrett Wilson Williams. As she captured her life, her children and grand children and The Way Things Were as she sees it today.

Acknowledgments

I would like to acknowledge the contributions of two special people, first of all to my grandmother Lizzie Robinson Garrett for her sincere words of encouragement and amazing power of influence and second to my mother, Josephine Robinson a successful mother and woman who in her own way inspired me to be all that I could be. I have so many friends, associates and family members to thank for their love and support. Thanks for helping me to tell my story in exactly the right words. Without all of you this manuscript world probably never have been written.